Creative
PATIOS

Tina Skinner

Schiffer Publishing Ltd

4880 Lower Valley Road, Atglen, PA 19310 USA

Designed by Bonnie M. Hensey
Cover Design by Bruce M. Waters
Type set in ZapfChan Bd BT/Aldine721 BT
ISBN: 0-7643-1278-2
Printed in China

Cover images: *Courtesy of Gappsi™, Inc., LaRosa Landscape Company, Inc.,* and *Superlight Block.*
Title page image: *Courtesy of Bomanite Corporation.*

Published by Schiffer Publishing Ltd.
4880 Lower Valley Road
Atglen, PA 19310
Phone: (610) 593-1777; Fax: (610) 593-2002
E-mail: Schifferbk@aol.com
Please visit our web site catalog at www.schifferbooks.com

In Europe, Schiffer books are distributed by
Bushwood Books
6 Marksbury Rd.
Kew Gardens
Surrey TW9 4JF England
Phone: 44 (0)181 392-8585; Fax: 44 (0)181 392-9876
E-mail: Bushwd@aol.com

This book may be purchased from the publisher. Include $3.95 for shipping. Please try your bookstore first. We are interested in hearing from authors with book ideas on related subjects.
You may write for a free catalog.

Courtesy of Portland Cement Association

Contents

Acknowledgments—4

Introduction—5

Not Just a Concrete Slab—10

    A Look at the New Materials—10

        Pavers—10

        Inprinted Concrete—16

How They're Made—20

    A Step-by-Step Guide to Installing Your Own Interlocking

        Paver Patio—22

Patios for Every Purpose—29

    The Entryway Patio and Front Porch—29

    Outdoor Rooms—38

    Perfect Around Pool, Tub, and Pond—58

    Dining Alfresco—86

On Many Levels—98

    Minimal Environmental Impact (and Investment)—116

    Tips on Decorating Your Patio—132

        Furnishings—132

        Creating a Focal Point—134

        Thinking Outside the Box—143

    Showplace of Great Projects— 159

Resource Guide—188

Acknowledgments

One need only read the rich resource guide at the back of the book to see who contributed to this project. It's a wonderful mix of manufacturers, industry organizations, and talented contractors and landscape designers.

I also owe special thanks to a husband who finds concrete inspiring; a man who happily accepted a Valentine's Day gift of his very own cement mixer, and as a result thinks me the ideal wife.

Even more credit goes to his mother, Marcia Sibol, who had her old patio completely redone in such a beautiful, inspiring way that my interest was sparked. Landscape designer David Rockwell took her old pavers and incorporated them in a new, expanded design. He cleaned some, and left some with their moss, all handsomely mixed in with new material. He included circular paver formations, and lighting that shines up old oak trees in the evenings and creates a wonderful effect. I dedicate this book to her.

The patio that inspired this book: a handsome blend of old and new.

When it comes to outdoor living, the trend is down. Moving away from elevated decks, homeowners are setting their sights lower, closer to the Earth, the garden, the dew. And yet free of it.

One reason for the patio's appeal is that it puts you closer to the garden you love and tend. Patios provide a view of the lawn and the great beyond, unadulterated by safety railings. Plus, they give you a level of privacy not found on an elevated deck or porch. Planter boxes, shrubs, and privacy screens easily conceal a patio, partially or completely, and create an outdoor sanctuary.

On the practical side, patios are virtually maintenance free, if properly installed. Depending on how you've furnished your patio, the only care required may be a regular sweeping.

Economics plays a role, too. A lot of people are moving away from decks because of the cost, according to Tony Catanzaro of Regency Landscape. It actually costs more per square foot — $17-25 per square foot versus $10-16 per square foot for a patio – plus you have a lot more maintenance, he says.

The primary reason why patios are gaining popularity, though, is new technology. New materials make patios far less expensive, and more readily available. Amazing things are happening in the decorative paving industry. Those old cracking cement slabs and crumbling brick patios are a thing of the past. New concrete technology has increased the durability of paving materials, and advances in coloring and imprinting make it possible to imitate virtually any surface – inexpensively. You might not be able to afford bluestone or slate, or maybe there are no bluestone or slate quarries within hundreds of miles – but you can have that look.

"Hardscaping is a major part of design, and people don't think about it until they are in their new houses," says contractor Larry Ring. "It's much better to use a patio – it's more private than using an elevated deck that doesn't allow you access to your whole backyard.

"The first question I ask people is what they are going to do with the patio," says Ring. "What kind of furniture they will use. From that we come up with a size. You need a minimum of twelve feet for a circular table."

The rule of thumb that Tony Catanzaro of Regency Landscape uses to determine scale for a patio is as follows: Divide the height of your roofline by two for the perfect width. Deviating too far from this formula will give you a patio that looks too small or too large for the house.

The most important rule of thumb in designing a patio for your home, though, is finding what you like. That's what this book is for. Here are hundreds of photos to thumb through, hundreds of design ideas to help you "hardscape" your environment. You can choose colors, textures, and shapes that appeal to you, as well as study furnishings and features that you'd like to incorporate in your outdoor living room. You'll see a broad sampling of both new and old materials, from high-tech concrete hardeners and coloring agents to classic, quarried stone, and learn the language you need to discuss these materials with designers and contractors.

If you want to initiate the neighborhood's most talked-about home improvement project, we've got lots of ideas for you. This book is littered with pool studded, multilevel, gazebo-clad patios fit for glitterati.

We don't stop with the backyard, either. Shown are projects that incorporate front and rear; wraparound "hardscapes" that tie front, back, and side yards together. Here are design ideas that announce, upon arrival, that this house is a step above the rest.

However, if you're watching your wallet, don't be daunted by the showplaces featured here. There are also simple, humble patio and walkway ideas. There's even a step-by-step guide if you're ambitious enough to do the work yourself.

These images will prove invaluable to people building their own home, who want to start off right. Even if you can't afford to lay pavers or use decorative concrete coatings right away, you can lay the foundation for them with your architect and contractor by leaving an appropriate concrete base to be capped in the future.

Though your vision of the perfect patio is complete with outdoor sound system and lighting, it may not all be in the budget this year. Nevertheless, the time to consider these future luxuries is in the initial planning stages, no matter how humble the initial patio project will be. You don't want to go back later and dig everything up just to install your wiring, says landscaper David Rockwell.

This book explores the many uses people put their patios to. Some serve as an outdoor living room or dining room, even a kitchen. Patios can be used to create a simple, sanitary skirt around the back of a home – a short transition from house to grass. They may ramble over an extensive lawn. Or they can extend the skirt of a pool and create places to sun and socialize.

Patios and "hardscape" can also be used to help tame and negotiate uneven terrain, or to maximize one's view of it. They can cap over shady areas where no grass will grow, or finish off a flat roof where formerly no people could go.

Use this book to help you visualize the patio of your dreams. Study colors and textures so you'll know what to look for when you go shopping; terminology so you'll know how to talk to your contractor. Use the resource guide to help you find the right manufacturer or installer to meet your needs. Properly installed, your new patio should serve you for many years. I hope you enjoy them!

The cat doesn't care whether or not this is real stone. Can you tell that it is imprinted concrete?
Courtesy of Patterned Concrete® Industries, Ltd.

A handsome parquet surface is created with a special cast and colored paver system. *Courtesy of Interlocking Concrete Pavement Institute*

Two tones of gray concrete pavers were used for walkway and stairs leading to this home. Curves accommodate rich flower beds. *Photography by Susan Palcko/Courtesy of Pavemaster*

Not Just a Concrete Slab

A Look at the New Materials

Pavers

Technology that was born to battle the cold in Canada has quickly spread around the globe. In the United States and Europe, enterprising companies are formulating new, more colorful, more durable takes on "brick" in concrete for both commercial and residential applications.

Pavers – cement or clay bricks formulated for ground contact – come in colors and interlocking shapes that will absolutely wow you. Plus, they are extremely durable and able to withstand a lot of abuse.

Ten to fifteen years ago, patios were concrete slabs or mortared bricks, says Larry Ring, who was trained as a mason. "We found, going back for maintenance, that these projects had problems. New construction is the worst because it settles."

With poor subgrade and compaction preparation, anything will settle, according to the ASCC Decorative Concrete Council, sometimes for decades.

"So today we use dry stack. There is no mortar. If for some reason, you have settling, you can go back and prop it up. You don't have to bust it up and lose product. You can pick it up and set it back down. Another thing is redesign. If you decide to put in a new project like a screened porch, we can pick the product up and use it again somewhere else," he said.

Dry set costs about double what asphalt does," says Larry Ring. "But your duration is a lot longer. It also increases the value of your home," the Maryland contractor said.

A significant increase, at that. Recent studies show that high-quality professional hardscaping adds 7 to 9 percent to the value of residential properties, according to *Landscape Architect and Specifier News*. So that investment in your leisurely outdoors lifestyle will have additional payoffs on down the line.

Dry-set concrete pavers, when arranged in this classic herringbone pattern, are one of the strongest surfaces available – able to withstand industrial machinery traffic. *Courtesy of Brick Association of the Carolinas*

Here's a classic look, and one contractor William Kirby has been trying to encourage. Kirby takes moss cuttings home and encourages them to grow. The moss gives new paving the feeling of age. Tips he's heard for helping it grow include putting yogurt in the cracks. *Courtesy of American Builders Associates, Inc.*

Pavers can be manufactured in any imaginable shape. Here a serrated edge gives these concrete pavers a unique and delightful fit. *Courtesy of Interlocking Concrete Pavement Institute*

11

Opposite page
Top: Pavers were placed in a creative parquet pattern for this patio. Dry set in the center, mortar was used along the border. *Courtesy of Pine Hall Brick*

Bottom: A close-up of mortared pavers, set in the "running band" pattern. *Courtesy of Pine Hall Brick*

Another classic pattern for brick pavers is the "basketweave." *Courtesy of Pine Hall Brick*

Special rounded edges in these "bull-nosed" pavers were designed to cap steps. *Courtesy of Pine Hall Brick*

13

Humble in dimension, this little 20 x 12-foot patio is grandiose in design. Two tones of square pavers were used to create a winding pattern with Southwestern flair. *Courtesy of American Builders Associates, Inc.*

A mosaic of pavers, used in a bank entryway in Maryland, demonstrates the incredible design versatility of this medium, even in combinations of only a few shades. *Courtesy of Interlocking Concrete Pavement Institute*

A two-tone design of diamond pavers creates a snakeskin-like effect for this entryway walk. A single layer of retaining wall block denotes the transition from planter beds to lawn. *Courtesy of L.A. Verruni Landscaping*

Imprinted Concrete

Concrete poured and set on site might fool you these days. Science and ingenuity are providing pigments and textures that are drop-dead gorgeous, and economical.

Imprinted concrete, though more expensive than straight concrete or asphalt, provides significant savings for homeowners who want the look of natural stone, slate, tile or other surfaces without having to pay for them.

Technological advances enable professional installers to provide upscale looks at affordable prices. Textures are created with rollers and stamps. Patterns are created using stencils. And colors can be created and highlighted using special release powders, pigments, and acid stains.

Color hardeners are applied over freshly placed concrete. Imprinting mats and texturing tools are then used to provide the appropriate texture. Additional coloring highlights can be applied later, followed by a sealer.

Staining creates uneven, variegated, or translucent color effects on concrete surfaces, much like the shadings of natural stone or the aged appearance of a timeworn patina. The stains become part of the concrete surface and only wear as the concrete wears.

The advantages, of course, revolve around cost. These are estimated at $5 to $11 per square foot. Time is also a factor – installation is generally faster than hand-laying pavers.

There are maintenance costs involved, as well. Acrylic sealers need to be reapplied every three to five years, depending on your installer's recommendations and the products used. Additionally, a homeowner will want to be careful to never expose their imprinted concrete to chemicals that might harm or stain the sealers. Also, chips to the surface may need to be repaired. However, you don't have to bother with weeds growing up through imprinted "cracks" or between "bricks."

For the durability of the imprinted concrete surface, it is important that the installer create an area that drains properly as well as excavating and installing a proper sub-grade base. Further, steel bars for reinforcement can be used within for additional strength. All concrete should meet minimum standards, according to the ASC Decorative Concrete Council and the American Concrete Institute.

Most product manufacturers train and license installers, and can recommend qualified contractors.

A roller was used to create the texture of stone. Pigment was hand-cast to add variation to this illusion in concrete. *Courtesy of Patterned Concrete® Industries, Ltd.*

The "stones" in this patio were individually accented with colors to match the real flagstone borders. *Courtesy of Patterned Concrete® Industries, Ltd.*

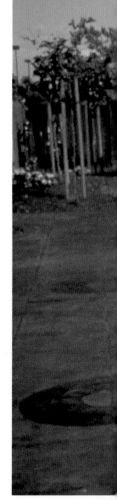

An intriguing series of looping dark graphic patterns in imprinted concrete was set into an oversize tile pattern to create focal points on this generous pool skirt. *Courtesy of Bomanite Corporation*

Showing the versatility of imprinted concrete, the joints in this patio have actually been grouted to duplicate the look of authentic slate. *Courtesy of Patterned Concrete® Industries, Ltd.*

A stunning star was created for this beach-front patio using acrylic cement coatings. *Courtesy of Sundek Products, Inc.*

A colorful star was created on concrete using a chemical/acid stain call Stain-Crete. *Courtesy of Increte Systems*

Laying pavers is a fairly simple process, though the work is arduous. Upon meeting with new clients, landscaper David Rockwell always stresses that a patio installation is a major construction project. A lot of earth gets moved and a property undergoes temporary upheaval. Grass is shorn off, dirt is piled high, and it can be unnerving. If you're doing it yourself, it can also be a lot of work.

Landscape designer Tony Catanzaro was called in to salvage a project gone wrong here. One major problem — set into a hillside, the patio drained toward the house. Major dirt was moved here, and packed away with lovely stone-capped retaining walls that also serve as seating. "A lot of filling and compacting took place," he said. Raised or sunken patios are jobs for heavy machinery, and, unless you're really confident, for proven professionals. *Courtesy of Regency Landscape*

A Step-by-Step Guide to Installing Your Own Interlocking Paver Patio

Laying pavers is easier than you might think, and the results can be beautiful and enduring. Following is advice from the Brick Association of the Carolinas for those who want to try their own hand at installing a paver patio or walkway. Remember, this is an abbreviated guide. The association suggests you consult with your brick supplier or a landscape professional when undertaking complex projects.

Association of the Carolinas
After the subsoil has been compacted, it's time to add the gravel. Although it may not be necessary for small or low-traffic areas, gravel will help keep your paved area level for years. *Photo by Rick Hovis/ Courtesy of Brick*

Opposite page
Top: For starters, a level site needs to be excavated, removing enough soil to allow for a thick layer of gravel (3-4 inches for a patio, 8 inches for a driveway), plus a 1 to 1-1/2 inch layer of sand or stone screenings, and the thickness of your selected pavers. *Photo by Rick Hovis/Courtesy of Brick Association of the Carolinas*

Bottom: The excavated area should extend about 6 inches beyond the area you plan to pave to provide an adequate foundation and allow for proper drainage. Also, you will want to slope the excavated site about 1/4-inch per foot (1" every 4'). Use a level with pipe, as shown, or boards to check the slope. Before applying any gravel, sand, or paving material, compact the subsoil layer either using a vibrating plate compactor or by allowing the area to stand through several rains or soakings with a hose. *Photo by Rick Hovis/Courtesy of Brick Association of the Carolinas*

Again, it's time to use a vibrating plate compactor, available in most equipment rental shops, to compress the gravel base. *Photo by Rick Hovis/Courtesy of Brick Association of the Carolinas*

Don't be tempted to compensate for an improperly compacted or un-level subsoil base during the sand and screeding step. Such an adjustment will ultimately result in an uneven surface and unwanted settling. *Photo by Rick Hovis/Courtesy of Brick Association of the Carolinas*

Level the sand or stone screenings with a heavy-duty rake. *Photo by Rick Hovis/Courtesy of Brick Association of the Carolinas*

Place two parallel lengths of 1-inch pipe on the gravel approximately 6-feet apart to serve as runners. Cover the sub-base with sand or stone screenings to a depth of 1-1/2" or less. Pull a 2x4 across the sand atop the two pipes, removing any excess material. Don't worry about any voids in the sand's surface, including those caused by the pipes. These can be hand-filled and troweled smooth as you lay your bricks. You'll want to work on freshly screeded sand and avoid walking on your leveled surface. If rain threatens before your work is completed, remember to keep your sand dry, using a plastic cover. *Photo by Rick Hovis/Courtesy of Brick Association of the Carolinas*

Edging can be done before or after laying the pavers. It is necessary to hold a no-mortar installation in place. If your selected pattern or plan involves a lot of brick cutting, edging is more easily and accurately accomplished afterwards, advises the Brick Association of the Carolinas.

Edging systems can consist of a run of bricks on-edge, trowel-finished concrete with backfill soil, or continuous plastic or metal retainers. The system shown is the patented Gappsi™ Edge Restraint System. Stakes are nailed through the long straps to hold the edge system in place. *Courtesy of Gappsi™, Inc.*

Lay pavers in your chosen pattern. If your paving is adjacent to a solid structure such as a wall, you'll want to work out from there. Set the pavers lightly on the sand, never pressing them or hammering them in. Every 4 feet or so, use a perpendicular string line to check your progress. If pavers are "lagging" behind the desired pattern, carefully insert a small screw driver and work them forward until they are in proper alignment. If they are running slightly ahead of the pattern, use a rubber mallet to nudge them into place. *Photo by Rick Hovis/Courtesy of Brick Association of the Carolinas*

Remember to stop six inches short of the originally excavated area to allow edging and drainage to extend beyond. Obviously it's easier if you choose a pattern which minimizes or eliminates cutting. If necessary, however, brick can be rough cut using a broad blade chisel and hammer. For finer cuts, a brick splitter or power saw with a masonry diamond blade will do the jobs. These are available at most equipment rental shops. *Photo by Rick Hovis/Courtesy of Brick Association of the Carolinas*

Sweep the bricks and then use a vibratory plate compactor to tamp from the perimeter inward, going over the surface at least twice until the surface is level to your satisfaction. *Photo by Rick Hovis/Courtesy of Brick Association of the Carolinas*

27

Spread a thin layer of jointing sand and use a stiff-bristle "street" broom to sweep and tamp it into the joints until they are filled. After sweeping, run the compactor across the surface for a final time. If cracks open up, sweep additional sand to fill them. Backfill around the perimeter with top soil and sod or seed. *Photo by Rick Hovis/Courtesy of Brick Association of the Carolinas*

The Entryway Patio and Front Porch

A small entryway patio serves its owners well in a friendly neighborhood where passersby often stop for a short chat with the homeowners. *Courtesy of David Rockwell & Associates, Inc.*

When a front porch is wanting, even a small patio can create a place to relax and watch the neighbors go by. Patterned bluestone was used for this gentle entryway. *Courtesy of Regency Landscape*

Two tones of gray were used for walkway and the entrance to this home. Curves accommodate rich flower beds. *Photography by Susan Palcko/Courtesy of Pavemaster*

Flagstones were used for an entryway patio to this home, creating a transitional area from a drive of brick pavers. *Courtesy of Marc Services, Inc.*

Entryway patios are very popular according to landscape designer Tony Catanzaro. Here the retaining wall can be used as a seat. "It's a welcoming patio, a very architectural thing to do," he says. *Courtesy of Regency Landscape*

A curved walk of terra-cotta-colored brick pavers winds from the driveway to an entryway patio, the front door, and around to the back of the house. In its infancy, the homeowner has plans for rich plantings around the walkways. *Courtesy of Marc Services, Inc.*

This walkway traverses the front of a home. An interesting square was inserted before the entrance to allow for a potted plant. The straight lines lend a formal air to the approach. *Courtesy of Glen-Gery Corporation*

Concrete can be colored and imprinted to create any type of stone. Here it was imprinted to imitate slate used on the streets of New Orleans, making for a classic front porch. *Courtesy of Patterned Concrete® Industries, Ltd.*

Wide steps lead to a decorative landing, all color keyed in pink and grey pavers. This is one of contractor Ralph Angelo's favorite projects. "We specialize in going over existing concrete slabs, or putting down new ones and topping them with pavers. Here the original concrete steps were covered with limestone overlay that's 2.5 inches thick."

An area beside a driveway was becoming overgrown and difficult for homeowners to handle. So they called in landscape designer David Rockwell to create something that required less maintenance. The result was a small patio area and stone steps amidst hearty perennials that require little attention. *Courtesy of David Rockwell & Associates, Inc.*

Outdoor Rooms

Following are hundreds of great ideas and technical tips for building the perfect patio for you and your family. Each image has ideas for surface materials and colors, as well as adornments such as furnishing ideas and built-in seating arrangements. Cooking stations are featured, as well as pool skirts. Gazebos and trellises are pictured along with fountains. Additionally, most of the pictures include landscaping ideas for assuring that your outdoor life-style features the best of the outdoors. Enjoy!

Mixed tones in the brick pavers create the impression that this pretty little patio has been part of the landscape for a long time. An elegant pergola and custom-built privacy screen are wonderful dressing. *Photo by Kim Kurian/Courtesy of Greenridge Landscaping*

Opposite page
Straight lines were avoided in this patio addition, with a curved wall defining the outer limits, following the lines set by a sturdy shade shelter. Charcoal-colored pavers create a contrast with the wood and cream tones of the home.
Courtesy of Superlight Block

A room outdoors is created with an extended
roofline and some columns. A "stone" floor of
imprinted concrete guarantees low maintenance
and cleanup time for this inviting hangout.
Courtesy of Patterned Concrete® Industries, Ltd.

Inside gives way gradually to outside with this arching overhang and a big skirt of concrete imprinted to look like classic flagstone. Pigment added to the concrete not only enhances the appearance, it makes the concrete stronger and harder, says Rose Higdon. *Courtesy of Patterned Concrete® Industries, Ltd.*

The texture on this patio resembles real brick pavers, but it was created using a 4x8-foot pattern imprinted on concrete. *Courtesy of Patterned Concrete® Industries, Ltd.*

Matching cement tabletops were created from stamped concrete to match the patio surface. *Courtesy of Patterned Concrete® Industries, Ltd.*

A pretty pink patio topped by a white wrought iron gazebo has a feminine, Florida feel. The parquet texture was created using acrylic cement coating and stencils over an existing concrete pad. *Courtesy of Sundek Products, Inc.*

A shade shelter and a matching privacy fence make this a bright yet cool place. For the surface, brick pavers were sand set in a herringbone pattern. *Courtesy of Sterling Landscape*

Columns and an extended roofline from the house create an indoor/outdoor living space, with sheltered eating areas close to the home, swimming area and beyond. Concrete pavers imitate stone. *Courtesy of Portland Cement Association*

Sparse, clean lines reflect the Arizona desert beyond, while a slatted roof helps protect those underneath from the harsh sun. *Photo by James Yochum/Courtesy of Louis Marson & Sons, Inc.*

This rambling concrete pad allows the homeowners to wander from the shelter of a shade arbor to the pleasing sight and sound of a fountain. *Courtesy of Portland Cement Association*

The bold lines of a modern home continue in a shadow-like patio extending into the lawn. Under the overhang, fieldstone was used for the patio surface, cement aggregate beyond. *Photos by James Yochum/Courtesy of Louis Marson & Sons, Inc.*

Stone is the look everyone wants, though it can be accomplished with a much smaller budget using concrete. Here a sheltered patio blends into pool skirt in an attractive "flagstone" pattern. *Courtesy of Portland Cement Association*

Latticework overhead creates an indoor/outdoor atmosphere. The area has been broken up into zones for plants and people, with a railing to define the outer boundary and underline a mountain view. *Courtesy of Portland Cement Association*

This patio was imprinted with a pattern called Sidewalk Slate. The texture for the pattern came right off the sidewalks of New Orleans. *Courtesy of Patterned Concrete® Industries, Ltd.*

This stamped cement patio resembles hand-placed cobblestones
accented by borders imprinted to look like natural stone.
Courtesy of Patterned Concrete® Industries, Ltd.

This patio was imprinted using a hexagon pattern and sealed with a colored wax to provide a uniform look. *Courtesy of Patterned Concrete® Industries, Ltd.*

At the request of the owners, the "stones" in this cement patio were accented by hand to match the stone in the columns. *Courtesy of Patterned Concrete® Industries, Ltd.*

Perfect Around Pool, Tub, and Pond

Hot tub and pool are disguised as a clear-blue pond, with a rock garden "island" on one side, and a clean patio "beach" of imprinted concrete on the other. A pavilion creates a shady place to gather and socialize. *Courtesy of Bomanite Corporation*

Warm tones and a rich pattern add interest to this pool skirt. *Courtesy of Gappsi™, Inc.*

Warm terra-cotta tone pavers were used for this pool skirt. *Courtesy of Pine Hall Brick*

Real stone is the look everyone is after. Here it is, native quarried stone for patio flagstones and a border wall. Stone was even used to create a diving board. *Courtesy of New York Quarries*

Boulders behind the pool add interest. The patio was color coordinated with a parquet pattern impressed on pigmented concrete.
Courtesy of Increte Systems

A fire pit in the foreground, and ground-level lighting around and inside the pool create an intriguing nighttime gathering place. The pool skirt is concrete, impressed and pigmented to imitate stone. *Courtesy of Increte Systems*

An inviting hot tub gets classic treatment with a surround of imprinted concrete to match the look of flagstones in the patio. Separate areas were created for the patio using brick pavers. *Courtesy of Bomanite Corporation*

A colorful diamond pattern was created for this pool skirt using square and special cast pavers. *Courtesy of Interlocking Concrete Pavement Institute*

Pressed concrete mimics natural stone for this pool skirt and patio. The chocolate tones of the concrete tint mimic the roof and complement pink stucco. *Courtesy of Portland Cement Association*

Vibrant colors were used for this swirling pool skirt design in pressed concrete. Bull-nosed pavers were used for the central pool surround. Besides adding beauty, the textures created in this concrete improve the footing and add an element of safety. *Courtesy of Portland Cement Association*

A circular wooden deck set upon a concrete slab becomes an enticing destination in this lovely backyard setting. Natural rock and flower beds break up the pool's shoreline, made all the more interesting by a complete lack of straight lines. A concrete pool skirt on the near side of the photo helps keep nature at bay. *Courtesy of Portland Cement Association*

Pressed concrete creates an unusual surface for this pool skirt. *Courtesy of Portland Cement Association*

This pool skirt is made up of pavers cast in a popular square-and-circle keyhole shape to create a wonderful interlocking pattern. *Courtesy of Portland Cement Association*

This phenomenal pool project combines Southwestern stucco architecture with classic Roman statuary. The center jewel, of course, is the sparkling blue swimming hole, surrounded by a patio sectioned by brick and cement slabs. *Photos by Visual Solutions/Courtesy of Louis Marson & Sons, Inc.*

An expansive outdoor space was created for this family, from the house-level patio to the pool skirt below.
Courtesy of Interlocking Concrete Pavement Institute

Barbell-shaped pavers add interest to this rich pool skirt and contrast with the white surround. *Courtesy of Portland Cement Association*

Interest was added to a rectangular pool and skirt with the addition of a half-circle area for seating, with a crescent of grass and a slightly elevated wall. *Courtesy of Portland Cement Association*

Real stone takes over where the "stones" of imprinted concrete end. *Courtesy of Increte Systems*

Shade shelters create an indoor/outdoor environment around this intriguing pool-scape. The patio surface is impressed concrete. *Courtesy of Increte Systems*

Three like-colored pavers create beautiful rows around a pool. *Courtesy of Gappsi™, Inc.*

A lovely brick paver surround makes this blue pool and hot tub seem an oasis. A raised area behind the hot tub both creates a perch for sunbathers and swimmers and hides the pool pump. *Courtesy of Gappsi™, Inc.*

Pavers in pleasing earth tones surround an oasis of blue water in the Arizona desert. *Courtesy of Superlight Block*

It looks like someone puzzled long and hard to fit together thick flagstones for this pool skirt. In fact, the "stones" are imprinted concrete. A nice touch is the natural stone used along the steps and bordering the walk. The small patio beyond is also imprinted concrete, made to resemble real brick. *Courtesy of Patterned Concrete® Industries, Ltd.*

Gray-colored keystone pavers are a nice complement to sparkling blue pool water. *Courtesy of Regency Landscape*

Imprinted concrete was colored to match this stucco home. *Courtesy of Increte Systems*

A pool takes on the aura of tropical lagoon, with palm trees for shade and stacks of natural stone. Blending in, imprinted concrete creates a pool skirt that seems like natural sandstone. *Courtesy of Bomanite Corporation*

Stamped concrete in terra-cotta tones give a warm surround to the cool pool, and ties in with the tile roofed, Mediterranean-style home. *Courtesy of Bomanite Corporation*

Here's a home for lovers of the outdoors. The home wraps around three sides of the backyard so that lots of rooms can look out. And they have a great view! A patio drops away from the house toward a pool, with sand-colored, slate-like imprinted concrete to match the house and contrasting concrete steps and retaining material. *Courtesy of Bomanite Corporation*

The typical pool skirt tends to create a desert-like environment. Here, however, a residential backyard becomes the kind of paradise most people fly to the tropics to visit. A shady bamboo pavilion, a rock garden, and unusual pool and hot tub design help create a blue lagoon-like retreat and break up the concrete surround. *Courtesy of Portland Cement Association*

Opposite page
Bottom: These homeowners wanted to mimic nature when they designed this pool to blend into the landscaping. Stone cap edges enhance the effect. A concrete surround and walkway is divided into flagstone shapes and given multi-levels to achieve the effect of a wooded path. *Courtesy of Portland Cement Association*

A broad swath of concrete pavers in a herringbone pattern were laid around this enticing pool. The rich earth tones add to the attraction. *Courtesy of Portland Cement Association*

An elevated patio keys in with the pool skirt via matching pavers set in a simple yet elegant parquet pattern. *Courtesy of Portland Cement Association*

Mortared bull-nosed pavers were used for the lip around the pool. Beyond that, concrete was tinted, placed, and pressed to resemble stone blocks. *Courtesy of Portland Cement Association*

A seam in the concrete is the only giveaway that this walkway and pool skirt weren't made from blocks of stone. *Courtesy of Portland Cement Association*

It's a kitchen/dining room outdoors. The barbecue allows the owners to prepare food outside, and the furnishings make it inviting to stay outside to eat. A double border was created for this patio in earth-toned pavers. *Courtesy of the Masonry Institute Inc.*

An "eye" was inset into the border around this patio, creating a focal point, here garnished with a potted shrub. Round tables and benches were chosen to complement the circular patterns in the pavers. *Courtesy of Interlocking Concrete Pavement Institute*

Opposite page
Which side of the windows would you rather be on? Stone and brick were created from concrete for this inviting little back patio. The concrete was poured on site and then imprinted or stamped, with the slab formation creating better integrity for the surface. *Courtesy of Patterned Concrete® Industries, Ltd.*

These homeowners wanted to seat 10-12 people on their patio, and to create an area that tied the driveway in with the backyard. Areas near the house were reserved for plantings, softening the effect of this sprawling hardscape. *Courtesy of Cedar Ridge Landscape*

Faux bricks were laid using stencils and an acrylic cement coating. *Courtesy of Sundek Products, Inc.*

Here are homeowners who like to be outdoors. Their terraced patio cascades down four levels into the garden. *Courtesy of Patterned Concrete® Industries, Ltd.*

A lot of earth was moved for this project to help build up a foundation for this raised patio behind a new home. It makes for a more comfortable transition from inside to out, and it creates a platform from whence to sit and enjoy the view. *Courtesy of L.A. Verruni Landscaping*

A bi-level patio was created in colored concrete, stamped to look like slate. A pedestrian gets warning to step up by additional concrete simulating the look of red bull-nose (rounded-end) pavers. *Courtesy of Bomanite Corporation*

The well-appointed patio might well include a brick oven, a fireplace to gather round on a chilly evening, a wet sink, even an electrical outlet or two for television or stereo entertainment. Here are a few fine examples. *Courtesy of IXL Industries, Ltd.*

Here it is, every red-blooded American (or Australian, or ...)'s dream. A great big barbecue station, the focal point at the perimeter of this patio. Brick pillars and border add interest to this private brick-and-mortar complex in South Carolina. *Photo by Jeff Amberg/Courtesy of Brick Association of the Carolinas*

Long pavers were used for this patio, including a semicircular area set aside solely for the outdoor chef. *Courtesy of the Masonry Institute Inc.*

This large patio was designed for entertaining. A barbecue was built in, with range and oven, under the gazebo. Antiqued/tumbled pavers were installed to give the cobblestones a timeless appearance. *Photos by Kim Kurian/Courtesy of Greenridge Landscaping*

This raised platform strikes an accord between house level and the garden beyond. Poised between, a table waits for company at the next meal. *Courtesy of IXL Industries, Ltd.*

Two tiers and stairways defined in gentle arches add grace to this patio. Pressed and pigmented concrete creates the effect of natural stone. *Courtesy of Portland Cement Association*

Circles and fans were designed into this patio for visual interest. The dark red creates a pleasing contrast against the golden shades in the home and new shade shelter. *Courtesy of Interlocking Concrete Pavement Institute*

The architect on this house project got excited when he saw trellis work being installed by landscaper Larry Ring in the front of the house, so he incorporated the trellis squares into the roofline in back. Below, a patio of Cambridge cobble pavers fills a three-sided courtyard. *Courtesy of Cedar Ridge Landscape*

97

On Many Levels

Properly planned, patios can actually help correct difficult landscapes. A patio isn't always a one-level little platform on flat ground behind your home. It can rise and fall with the landscaping, actually helping you access more of your lawn and garden. Further, a patio can really maximize the built-in advantages of hilltop locations; without need of railings, a ground-level patio offers no obstruction to a great view. Where there are no hills, elevation can be added. Retaining walls can raise a patio, or a wall around the patio can provide an aura of privacy. Remember, too, that a patio doesn't always have to be in contact with the soil. They are especially charming up on a roof.

Raised patios by the house curve gracefully down to pool side, with matching concrete borders that mimic slate and tie the whole together. *Courtesy of Bomanite Corporation*

Field stone was put to work to hold back nature on this steep hillside, and concrete was colored and stamped to blend in on the walking surfaces.
Courtesy of Bomanite Corporation

This bi-level raised patio seems to spill into the yard. *Courtesy of Marc Services, Inc.*

This cement patio was stamped and stained to resemble natural flagstones, bordered by plain cement. The design carries through in the attached pool deck. *Courtesy of Patterned Concrete® Industries, Ltd.*

Concrete keeps it simple in terms of cleanup and usable space in the back yard. Here two surfaces were used – concrete was patterned to look like flagstones for the upper level and hot tub skirt, and the lower level is poured concrete in a matching color. *Courtesy of Patterned Concrete® Industries, Ltd.*

An interesting patio and pool skirt were created using contrasting colors.
A retaining wall was built to help level a raised area for an upper patio.
Photography by Susan Palcko/Courtesy of Pavemaster

Opposite page
A rich view of pool, a pretty creek, and pastoral
meadow was preserved with this terraced concrete
patio. The surface was enhanced with pigment and
imprinted to imitate cut stone. *Courtesy of Patterned
Concrete® Industries, Ltd.*

A retaining wall was used to create a patio area next to the home, and hold back a hill and built in pool beyond. *Courtesy of Regency Landscape*

Keystone retaining wall blocks create an intriguing wall around this patio, as well as a colorful border. *Courtesy of L.A. Verruni Landscaping*

Opposite page
Retaining walls create a beautiful backdrop while cutting out a level area for a skirt of patio behind this home, carpeted with pressed concrete. *Courtesy of Portland Cement Association*

A radiant pattern of imprinted concrete in a traditional brick-red color create a lively substructure here for a patio made special by raised flower beds and built-in concrete benches. *Courtesy of Bomanite Corporation*

Retaining walls and privacy walls are softened when space is left for soil and plantings.
Courtesy of IXL Industries, Ltd.

Retaining walls with spaces left open for plants are enormously popular in Europe. This image was taken at a showplace for a German paver manufacturer called Ehl. *Courtesy of Interlocking Concrete Pavement Institute*

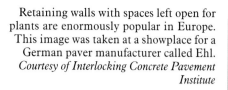

A mortared brick wall matches interlocking pavers on the patio. The wall creates a safety barrier for children, built-in seating for adults. *Courtesy of Pine Hall Brick*

Cut stone mirrors a natural stone wall beyond on this elevated patio and wall overlooking a quarry. *Courtesy of New York Quarries*

Stencils and pigmented cement hardeners were used to create this rooftop patio. *Courtesy of Increte Systems*

Different patterns and colors in imprinted concrete were used to create this stone-like walkway and patio overlooking a pond. *Courtesy of Bomanite Corporation*

Rough-hewn lumber and quarried rock create a fabulous, rustic wilderness retreat.
Courtesy of New York Quarries

A herringbone patterned patio narrows in two stages before dropping off to a path leading to a lake. *Courtesy of Pine Hall Brick*

Faux marble was created for this rooftop patio using a combination of acrylic cements and fiberglass. A simple wire barrier was strung up prevent someone from falling off while preserving the view. *Courtesy of Sundek Products, Inc.*

This cement "slate" pattern was imprinted on a diagonal for a dramatic effect. *Courtesy of Patterned Concrete® Industries, Ltd.*

This raised deck was constructed of concrete using stamps and color to create a permanent surface. The colors were chosen to enhance the imported slate stepping stones and the river rock foundation. A walkway makes a nice transition from patio to lawn, with spacing for green grass and moss. *Photo © Alan Bisson/Courtesy of Meidling Concrete, Inc.*

The effect of natural stone was sought for this log cabin's cement patio overlooking a lake. *Courtesy of Increte Systems*

Simplistic style – clean-cut lines of a concrete patio surround a single-lane lap pool amidst a straight, green lawn. The all-important waterfront view is unobstructed. The neighbors chose a similar look, with a pool set deep for diving rather than laps. *Courtesy of Bomanite Corporation*

A "stone" perch was created to overlook this beautiful vista. The "stones" are imprinted concrete, distorted slightly by a wide-angle lens. *Courtesy of Increte Systems*

Color variations were achieved using a combination of color hardener and chemical/acid stain. The curved effect was created by a wide angle lens on the camera. *Courtesy of Increte Systems*

Opposite page
Bluestone was wet set, adding impact to the natural colors. *Courtesy of LaRosa Landscape Company*

Minimal Environmental (and Economic) Impact

Like any home improvement book, this one is packed with examples of the most luxurious add-ons to be had. However, a patio can, and maybe should, be a simple thing. Here are some wonderful ideas to consider, whether you're worried about the investment, or whether you want a living space that leaves plenty of room for Mother Nature. There are examples here to suit both needs.

The homeowners wanted to screen off a view they didn't like from their bedroom, so they installed this miniature patio. "Neither thought they'd ever use it," says contractor Larry Ring. Still, the husband now likes to go there to smoke cigars, and his wife reads the newspaper there. *Courtesy of Cedar Ridge Landscape*

Simplicity at its finest, the stones in this walkway seem to have fallen into place all by themselves. At the end of this charming walk lies a fairy ring of stones, a little retreat behind a privacy fence in a highly populated area. *Courtesy of LaRosa Landscape Company, Inc.*

116

A retreat can be this simple — a tiny place carved out in brick pavers, where two people can sit in private conference out of doors. *Courtesy of LaRosa Landscape Company, Inc.*

A gardener's rest offers a retreat where one can enjoy the visual and fragrant fruits of their labor. *Courtesy of Tim R. S. Garland*

A sweet little circle is set as a stage for an intimate gathering of friends. *Courtesy of the Masonry Institute Inc.*

Opposite page
Top: Here's a secretive retreat, a small space carved out for one weary soul. The only adornments are a clean, flagstone floor and a comfy hammock amidst tall shade trees. *Courtesy of David Rockwell & Associates, Inc.*

Bottom: Concrete pavers were tumbled to prematurely age them and create this timeless little patio. *Courtesy of Portland Cement Association*

This family patio doubles as basketball court, with pigmented concrete laying a foundation for the game. *Courtesy of Patterned Concrete® Industries, Ltd.*

Opposite page
Simple, small, and yet elegant, this little patio pushes its way into a small yard with a distinct, classical air, aided by an antique fountain and cast-iron patio furniture. Concrete was stained to imitate terra-cotta tiles. *Courtesy of Patterned Concrete® Industries, Ltd.*

"This is my number one patio," says contractor Ralph Angelo. "Everyone loves that. Fifty percent of my work is what you see there. Using a simple brick border cuts costs dramatically. Almost all of my customers can afford this one. The concrete slab is reinforced with steel rod or rebar that is drilled into the house foundation every 24 inches. The slab sits on that steel foundation, not the ground. And we use a higher quality concrete to eliminate cracks." *Courtesy of Petriello Construction Corporation*

A retractable awning allows these new homeowners to create shade for their patio, because it will be years before the trees nearby mature. Potted plants help enhance the new landscaping. *Courtesy of L.A. Verruni Landscaping*

This little patio is a great place to sit with friends on a cool autumn evening. *Courtesy of L.A. Verruni Landscaping*

A combination deck/patio fills the "L" behind a home, with plantings positioned to optimize privacy. *Courtesy of Regency Landscape*

A strip of patio was created in concrete, stamped in a pattern designed to resemble slate. *Courtesy of Patterned Concrete® Industries, Ltd.*

A very small backyard becomes a recreation area as well as a garden. Multi-toned "Keystone" shaped pavers add interest. *Courtesy of Interlocking Concrete Pavement Institute*

Lush foliage and a raised deck create a privacy screen around a ground-level patio, giving it an aura of seclusion. The concrete surface incorporates colored tint for a flagstone effect. Planter beds were built with wide walls to achieve additional seating opportunities. *Courtesy of Portland Cement Association*

Architect Chris Craiker of San Rafael, California, took advantage of every inch in this small back yard, creating a private place with a slatted redwood fence, and creating a natural feel underfoot with enormous stones. *Courtesy of California Redwood Association*

By spacing concrete "stones" a little farther apart, and filling the spaces with rich soil instead of nutrient-poor sand, this patio designer created a place for a little grass. Though it needs periodic mowing, this combination of hard- and soft-scape is pleasant to the eye, and creates a smooth transition between patio and lawn. *Courtesy of Interlocking Concrete Pavement Institute*

Nature was only slightly improved upon here, with stepping stones forming a path and providing footrests before simple benches. The magnificent Asian-inspired redwood gate was designed and crafted by Julian Hodges of Emeryville, California. *Courtesy of California Redwood Association*

Pavers manufactured with openings allow for a mixed hard- and soft-terrain with several environmental advantages: runoff is reduced and sunlight radiant heat is absorbed, which is better for the environment. Plus, it's pleasant to share outdoor space with nature. *Courtesy of Interlocking Concrete Pavement Institute*

A steep drop from home to backyard was conquered in stages – first with a deck, finally with this inviting raised patio behind a rock retaining wall. Plantings around the half-circle perimeter create an illusion that one is sitting at ground level. *Courtesy of Regency Landscape*

Here the homeowners started with an overlay project to cover up an older concrete walk. The pink and gray pattern was continued with a walkway around the house to a small patio in the back.
Courtesy of Petriello Construction Corporation

Two levels were incorporated into this patio created from pigmented concrete pressed to imitate stone. The shape and elevation create a perfect backyard stage for barbecues and family parties. *Courtesy of GT Concrete & Masonry*

Small but sweet, this little outdoor space gets a wallop of class in combined materials — a brick paver border around natural stone slabs. *Courtesy of LaRosa Landscape Company, Inc.*

Matching pavers and retaining wall blocks were used for this wraparound walkway and patio. The yard beyond is accessed via built-in stairs. *Photography by Susan Palcko/Courtesy of Pavemaster*

A little bit of patio adds a lot of outdoor living. This patio is little more than a skirt for a home with a very small backyard, yet it creates spaces for dining, for stretching one's legs and enjoying the fresh air, or for a quiet seat outdoors in the garden. *Courtesy of Portland Cement Association*

The urban backyard needs to be fully utilized. Here an attractive design marries concrete flatwork with pavers in a patchwork quilt decorated with flower beds. *Courtesy of Portland Cement Association*

130

Here's a setting that's hard to beat, overlooking a pond. Stone retaining walls were built to create raised planting beds and give one a feeling of seclusion. Piecing the patio surface together from different-shaped stones helps provide a sense of natural setting. *Courtesy of Vengeance Creek Stone*

Art imitates nature: A nautilus effect was created by laying a thick slab of concrete in an rough-sided mold, placing a stencil on top, and broadcasting pigmented hardener into the squares left showing. *Courtesy of Portland Cement Association*

Tips on Decorating Your Patio

Several key things will help set your patio apart – the furnishings you chose and the focal points you create – water features, statuary, landscaping. So we've shared a few nice examples here, and throughout the book. To create a real compliment-magnet on any scale or budget, though, you're going to want to think outside the box. In this chapter there are dozens of examples of people who have cut corners, creating well-rounded patios with interesting shapes. It might take a little more time, but if you break away from the standard rectangle slab we traditionally associate with patios, you're going to find yourself with a neighborhood masterpiece.

Furnishings

Natural sandstone pavers were set with mortar to cover an existing concrete pad. Furnished with teak and potted flowers, the patio became an instant showplace. *Courtesy of Sterling Landscape*

Opposite page
Set in a herringbone pattern, this mortared brick patio forms a flowing skirt around this home, providing a tidy area for outdoor dining and entertainment. A wrought iron picnic set completes a classic scene. *Courtesy of the Masonry Institute Inc.*

Here's a patio owner who knows how to decorate. Matching pillows and pottery and potted plants combine for a most pleasing effect on this patio.
Courtesy of David Rockwell & Associates, Inc.

Wicker and wrought iron are the two classic choices for patio furnishings. Here a casual combination of the two is absolutely charming. Landscaping creates a private patio built of concrete pavers. *Courtesy of Sterling Landscape*

Affordable and cheerful, patio sets with table, chair, and umbrellas are widely sold in stores today. Imprinted, textured, and colored concrete was used to create two levels of patio and steps in a matching color. *Courtesy of Bomanite Corporation*

A natural look was wanted for this patio, and achieved with blonde sandstone pavers mortar set on a concrete pad. A graceful entry to the backyard was created with hand-hewn stone steps leading from the home. The outdoor cooking area was likewise treated with sandstone to incorporate it into the design. *Courtesy of Sterling Landscape*

A pillared gazebo creates a classical focal point for this sprawling patio of imprinted concrete in a slate pattern. *Courtesy of Bomanite Corporation*

A classic white fountain creates the centerpiece for this expansive patio, with imprinted concrete in a brick pattern extending from the middle in a radiant grid pattern. Formal gardens beyond are an appropriate transition from hard to soft landscaping. *Courtesy of Bomanite Corporation*

Stamped concrete "slate" creates a walkway around a circular fountain feature. *Courtesy of Bomanite Corporation*

Pavers skirt a like-colored brick home and gently circle a bronze fountain. *Courtesy of Interlocking Concrete Pavement Institute*

A back garden terrace is small in size, rich in design. Split pavers form a running bond pattern inside the octagon's border, and a square cement slab creates a central motif. *Courtesy of Sterling Landscape*

A wooden retaining wall helps hold back a steep hillside crowned with woods. Below, a pleasing palate of gray pavers and a matching retainer wall form a circular patio area, crowned by a wooden shade shelter. *Courtesy of David Rockwell & Associates, Inc.*

140

Fresh pavers in a basket-weave pattern with a running border have been lightly adorned with potted plants and an arbor entryway. *Photo by Kim Kurian/Courtesy of Greenridge Landscaping*

Textured concrete creates a cozy perch lake side. Potted plants underline the view and mark the edge of the patio's territory. *Courtesy of Portland Cement Association*

A small table for gathering, garnished with a vase of fresh flowers, serves as invitation. This intimate little patio wasn't made from flagstones, as it appears, but stamped concrete. *Courtesy of Portland Cement Association*

Beautiful slate gray and blue flagstones of cast-in-place concrete create an idyllic party place, complete with a central water fountain and a host of flowers. *Courtesy of Bomanite Corporation*

142

There isn't a straight line on this patio, though a perfect circle was created in concrete imprinted to imitate oversized flagstones. The size of the flagstones helps create an illusion of more space. This unique project complements the stucco home it was added to. *Courtesy of Patterned Concrete® Industries, Ltd.*

A short pathway leads one into the landscape where three interlocking circles create congregation points. Rocks at the far side define the transition from hardscape to greenery, and offer natural seating, too. *Courtesy of American Builders Associates, Inc.*

Interlocking circles create a graceful backyard retreat. *Courtesy of Gappsi*™, *Inc.*

A circular corner in this house is mirrored in the patio below. Landscape designer Tony Catanzaro worked with the home's design to create this flowing patio layout. *Courtesy of Regency Landscape*

A lot of patio was desired by these homeowners, including a skirt for a sizable in-ground pool. To keep it economical and relatively maintenance free, concrete was used. To increase its beauty, central portions of the patio were pigmented and pressed to imitate fieldstone. The contrast in colors also works as a safety system, a visual cue to pedestrians about changes in level. *Courtesy of GT Concrete & Masonry*

Circular steps are mirrored in two gentle curves in the patio perimeter. Contrast was created between the clean white of pure concrete and a central area that was pigmented and stamped to imitate flagstone. *Courtesy of GT Concrete & Masonry*

A fascinating scalelike pattern is created in pavers, here used for a curving walkway and adjoining patio. *Photography by Susan Palcko/ Courtesy of Pavemaster*

The soft outline of this imprinted concrete patio is mimicked in the landscaping beyond. *Courtesy of Patterned Concrete® Industries, Ltd.*

A concrete slab is made distinct with pigment and texture. In addition, there were no straight edges incorporated into this design, which is essentially two patios linked together. *Courtesy of GT Concrete & Masonry*

Intimacy is a fine thing to aspire to in an outdoor "room." Scale should be based, in part, on how many people will utilize the space. *Courtesy of Regency Landscape*

Stamped concrete imitates stone in this patio of descending circles. Natural stone was used for the steps down to the yard, and river stone for flower bed borders. *Courtesy of GT Concrete & Masonry*

A half-moon staircase becomes a design element on this expansive patio. Cast in the same concrete color, stairs and patio surface imitate stone. Stamped concrete can be placed over existing concrete foundations. *Courtesy of Patterned Concrete® Industries, Ltd.*

Square brick pavers radiate from a central millstone pedestal. The sprawling patio has been furnished with wooden arbor and Adirondack-style chairs. *Photo by Dennis Nodine/ Courtesy of Brick Association of the Carolinas*

Opposite page
Stone steps and surface create an inviting entryway, except this isn't really stone. It's concrete that was imprinted to look like stone. The railing, likewise, is a solid structure of concrete. *Courtesy of Patterned Concrete® Industries, Ltd.*

Seen from above and beside, this patio is a beautiful melt of circular paver patterns. *Courtesy of Portland Cement Association*

Rambling "flag-stones" of pressed concrete create a rambling patio area that flows past flower beds and under a shady archway. *Courtesy of Portland Cement Association*

Circular stone steps lead away from home and pool to a garden beyond. *Courtesy of David Rockwell & Associates, Inc.*

Circling and stretching the length of this home, a patio of brick
pavers creates several gathering areas, with fire at either end in the
forms of a clay oven and a propane barbecue. *Courtesy of LaRosa
Landscape Company, Inc.*

Tucked neatly into the "L" of a rancher, this little patio feels like an outdoor room. A larger expanse of the soft-colored pavers beyond expands the space for bigger parties. *Courtesy of LaRosa Landscape Company, Inc.*

Interlocking fans and circles are popular patterns in pavers. Here the effect is created using a less-expensive stencil and pigmented sealer process. *Courtesy of Artcrete, Inc.*

Steps and a shade shelter define the decline between home and pool side patio. Rocks help soften the edges. Antiqued cobblestones were used for a softened effect. *Courtesy of Superlight Block*

These homeowners gave artist Giuseppe Abbrancati free reign around their wooded home to ornament their exterior with an exquisite driveway, entry, and an amazing rear patio. The patterns are made all the more striking by the incorporation of green accents. *Courtesy of Gappsi™, Inc.*

Building up a patio like this takes a whole lot of earth moving. The result, however, is spectacular. Here wooden timbers and railing create a deck-like atmosphere for a wonderful stage of brick pavers. This enormous patio includes raised planter beds to create an illusion that one is sitting at ground level, and provides different areas for congregating, cooking, and other activities. *Courtesy of Regency Landscape*

Under this concrete patio is usable space for storage and an indoor archery range. To create this space, the deck and patio were built directly on the foundation walls, waterproofing was applied to pressure treated wood and the concrete was poured, then stamped. An ashlar slate pattern was chosen for the stamp to contrast with the Montana River Rock used on the foundation and for planter boxes. *Photo © Alan Bisson/ Courtesy of Meidling Concrete, Inc.*

A retaining wall of Versa-Lok block creates an elevated patio and planters. A circle pattern was created for a focal area in red and gray cobblestone pavers, with a matching walk leading to the front of the house. *Courtesy of Cedar Ridge Landscape*

Retaining wall blocks create a rocklike divider between upper and lower levels of this patio, punctuated by genuine boulders. Pavers in various hues and sizes were used for the surface.
Courtesy of Superlight Block

166

An amazing layout was created for these homeowners by artist Giuseppe Abbrancati. A rose graces the entryway patio. At the driveway entrance, a three-dimensional effect is created from two colors of paver. Natural sandstone was inset in the corners of this perfectly square design. *Courtesy of Gappsi™, Inc.*

These ambitious homeowners created an impressive walkway for their private property. They installed over three semi-tractor trailer loads of brick pavers to create winding paths that are color-coordinated to match their Victorian home, according to contractor Andrew Robinson. *Photos by Kim Kurian/Courtesy of Greenridge Landscaping*

An old cracked concrete patio was replaced with this graceful expanse of slate-blend cobblestone pavers that were tumbled, or distressed, to create a classic look. An existing wall of Maryland flagstone traces the perimeter and defines the walk-up to the pool area.
Courtesy of Cedar Ridge Landscape

Imprinted and textured concrete creates a meandering walkway between home and pool, with places for planting flowers, or oneself, in the sun. The broken lines of the borders are a fascinating architectural addition to the landscape. *Courtesy of Bomanite Corporation*

A concrete drive, walkway, and patio were created using an unusual stamped pattern for an Art Deco effect. Matching steps cascade down toward the waterfront. *Courtesy of Bomanite Corporation*

171

Two distinct areas were created for outdoor living here. There is a wonderful flagstone terrace next to the building, with a gate to the driveway that makes this a rear entrance to the home. Steps descend to a deck in the garden, with built-in bench seating. *Courtesy of the Masonry Institute Inc.*

Concrete was pigmented to imitate tiles for this clean and classy, neatly contained little patio. *Courtesy of Portland Cement Association*

A pool and hot tub seemed sheltered from soil by a broad skirt of stamped concrete and protected from curious eyes by handsome walls crowned by white molding. *Courtesy of Bomanite Corporation*

A back doorway leads one down a series of steps and stops, and across a bridge paved in concrete stamped to imitate stone. *Courtesy of Bomanite Corporation*

Almost Aztec by moonlight, this columned shade shelter forms the far wall for a dramatic backyard pool. Fountains stream water into the deep end, and above, a sunken hot tub allows one to overlook the cooler waters. *Photos by Brett Drury/ Courtesy of Louis Marson & Sons, Inc.*

For those who use their backyards a lot, a lot of concrete is a good thing. Here pressed concrete creates a warm "stone" surface for the pool skirt and hot tub surround, walkways, and an outdoor fireplace and cook center. *Courtesy of Portland Cement Association*

These homeowners wanted their home to be unique within a new residential development. Part of that improvement included using concrete brick pavers for their entryway walk. The backyard was also well appointed, with a remarkable small patio/dining area adorned with a compass of hand-cut pavers. A partial skirt of pavers was installed around the pool, and areas were filled with river stones and slate steps to help keep down costs. *Courtesy of David Rockwell & Associates, Inc.*

An expansive driveway was created here for a homeowner who entertains. The back entry, however, was kept to an intimate scale, where imprinted concrete mimics the fieldstone in the home. *Courtesy of Bomanite Corporation*

Sand-colored concrete in a random pattern imitates slate in this rambling patio/walkway. *Courtesy of Bomanite Corporation*

For this impressive home of brick and stone, nothing short of the look of rich flagstones (actually concrete) would do for the entryway. The walk up was made all the more enticing with a bridge topped by turtle planters. *Courtesy of Bomanite Corporation*

Pond and patio fill the backyard of a water-loving family, linked by patio and matching walkway. Additionally, a small patio off a side door was created for a semiprivate retreat. *Courtesy of David Rockwell & Associates, Inc.*

All the classic elements were combined for this backyard paradise – water, fire, earth, and air. A lit waterfall across sky blue tiles is an aural and visual focal point for this place, when the grill isn't fired up. The surface was created from slip brick mortar set in a herringbone pattern over an existing concrete pad. *Courtesy of Sterling Landscape*

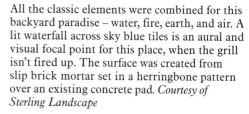

A pond of rippling water, a bridge as invitation, a place for fire on a cool evening — this is a place that wows a lot of quiet human company. *Courtesy of LaRosa Landscape Company, Inc.*

Paver edges were softened, stones lined up in this artful combination of texture and color. Stone risers lead to a shaded shelter and hot tub.
Courtesy of LaRosa Landscape Company, Inc.

A plain old patio would be, well, too plain behind an exotic home like this one. The landscape architect chose to caste long strips of diamond-shaped patterns imprinted in concrete away from the structure, creating a shadow-like effect. *Courtesy of Bomanite Corporation*

This driveway and patio are so handsome you might hesitate to park here. Artist Giuseppe Abbrancati designed color shifts and outlined areas to help break up the expanse of space and to direct traffic flow around a central circle, suggesting areas to be left open for pedestrian traffic closest to the house. Landscaping limits vehicles from family areas beyond. *Courtesy of Gappsi™, Inc.*

Resource Guide

American Builders Associates, Inc.
540 Westwood Avenue
River Vale, NJ 07675
201-722-8794/Fax: 722-1457
Company president William Kirby has been installing concrete pavers in New Jersey and New York since 1985, working on large commercial projects as well as custom-designed residential applications. He is trained and certified as an ICPI interlocking paving contractor, an Anchor Paving Stone Installer, and a Keystone Retaining Wall Builder.

Artcrete, Inc.
5812 Hwy. 4 94
Natchitoches, LA 71457
318-379-2000/Fax: 379-1000
artcrete@cp-tel.net
www.artcrete.com
Artcrete manufactures stencils and products for decorative concrete under the name Faux Brick. The company has been in business for 14 years, and is represented on every continent except Greenland and the poles.

Bomanite Corporation
P.O. Box 599
Madera, CA 93639
559-673-2411/Fax: 673-8246
www.bomanite.com
e-mail: bomanite@bomanite.com
Established in 1955, Brad Bowman developed the Bomanite process of imprinting concrete. In 1970, Bomanite Corporation was established to develop a national market and installation standard for his technique. There are now 114 franchise operations in the United States and Canada, and more than 250 various types of international licensees in 66 countries worldwide.

Brick Association of the Carolinas
8420 University Executive Park Dr.
Suite 800
Charlotte, NC 28262
800-622-7425/Fax: 704-510-0042
www.gobrick.com
This trade organization represents 14 brick manufacturers in North and South Carolina, where one out of every four bricks made in the United States is manufactured. The association is dedicated to promoting brick as the preferred building material for home and commercial construction and provides a wide array of educational and technical services for home buyers, builders, masons, and architects.

Cedar Ridge Landscape
4701 Long Green Road
Glen Arm, MD 21057
410-592-7119
President Larry Ring has been in business since 1980, creating residential and commercial landscaping. He is a full-service company, offering plantings, hardscapes, and accessories such as fences, decks, benches, trellis, garden structure, boulders, and ponds.

California Redwood Association
405 Enfrente Drive, Suite 200
Novato, CA 94949
415-382-0662/Fax: 382-8531
www.calredwood.org
This nonprofit trade association offers idea-starting, how-to, and specification information about redwood products and projects – decks, fences, siding, and paneling.

Decorative Concrete Council
7824 South Adams Street
Darien, IL 60561
630-852-5505/Fax: 630-960-9101
plrgraphix@aol.com
www.decorativeconcretecouncil.org
A council within the American Society of Concrete Contractors, the Decorative Concrete Council works within the industry to advance the quality and use of decorative concrete systems.

Gappsi™, Inc.
311 Veterans Memorial Highway
Commack, NY 11725
631-543-1177/Fax: 543-1188
info@gappsi.com
www.gappsi.com
Owner Giuseppe Abbrancati brought his artistry and over 17 years of experience in Europe to bear when he established his company. He is the inventor of what he calls "the most reliable edge restraint system in the industry," and he has created and patented his own paver shapes for exclusive manufacture. His work has won numerous awards.

Glen-Gery Corporation
1166 Spring Street
Wyomissing, PA 19610-6001
610-374-4011/Fax: 374-1622
gg@glengerybrick.com
www.glengerybrick.com
Glen-Gery operates ten manufacturing facilities and 15 sales offices and has over 850 distributors throughout the United States. The product line includes extruded, machine molded, authentic handmade and glazed facebrick, as well as brick paving units, pool copings, and a complete assortment of brick shapes.

Greenridge Landscaping
14 Minnesota Road
Carbondale, IL 62901
618-549-6165/Fax: 457-4367
arobin@midwest.net
Landscape contractor Andrew Robinson has more than 20 years of experience. He specializes in custom residential landscaping.

GT Concrete & Masonry
25871 Wiseman
Roseville, MI 48066
810-450-2407/Fax: 773-4619
tarnata@aol.com
www.gtconcrete.com

Increte Systems
8509 Sunstate St.
Tampa, FL 33634
813-886-8811/Fax: 886-0188
www.increte.com
Increte Systems specializes in decorative concrete systems and products, including stamped concrete, architectural wall systems, concrete coloring and stain systems, and decorative concrete overlays.

Interlocking Concrete Pavement Institute
1444 I Street NW, Suite 700
Washington, D.C. 20005-2210
202-712-9036/Fax: 408-0285
icpi@icpi.org
www.icpi.org
The Interlocking Concrete Pavement Institute (ICPI) is an autonomous association representing the interlocking concrete paving industry in North America. Membership is open to producers, contractors, suppliers, and consultants. As the industry voice, the membership represents a majority of the concrete paver production in North America.

IXL Industries, Ltd.
Clay Products Division
P.O. Box 70
Medicine Hat, AB TIA 7E7
Canada
403-502-1486/Fax: 526-7680
www.ixlbrick.com
Known as "The Brick People," IXL is versatile, supplying a wide variety of colors, textures, and sizes of brick for commercial, institutional, and residential projects. It is a family owned company in its third generation.

LaRosa Landscape Company, Inc.
10950 North Buntrock Avenue
Mequon, WI 53092
262-242-9092/Fax: 242-5236
larosa@larosalandscape.com
www.larosalandscape.com
LaRosa combines design and construction with maintenance and lawn care services for full client care. The company promotes an artistic approach to design, and employs award winning landscape architects Tim Garland and Chris Miracle toward that end.

Marc Services, Inc.
316 Hebron Road
Andover, CT 06232
860-742-2812
President Marc LaLonde has been in business about 11 years. He is ICPI certified and an authorized Unilock installer. He specializes in hardscaping, including pavers, flagstone, and bluestone installations.

Louis Marson & Sons, Inc.
7526 East Camelback Road
Scottsdale, AZ 85251
480-946-4100/Fax: 423-7445
marson@primenet.com
Louis Marson & Sons, Inc. is a residential and commercial construction and development company which has been family owned since 1952, incorporated in 1973. It provides services in residential, commercial, industrial and site work projects.

Masonry Institute Inc.
4853 Cordell Avenue
Penthouse One
Bethesda, MD 20814-3031
301-652-0115/Fax: 907-4922
www.brickblockandtrowel.org
John F. Cissel, Executive Director
Founded in 1955, The Masonry Institute, Inc. is the oldest regional masonry trade association. It promotes the use of masonry products in the Washington, D.C., metropolitan area.

Meidling Concrete, Inc.
12411 E. Empire Ave.
Spokane, WA 99215
509-924-7180/Fax: 927-1368
www.meidlingconcrete.com
A woman-owned business since 1990, the company is 45 years old. All phases of concrete construction, specializing in residential and commercial application of color embossed concrete and staining and other specialty finishes.